FREEDOM SONG

THE STORY OF HENRY "BOX" BROWN

By **SALLY M. WALKER**

Illustrated by **SEAN QUALLS**

HARPER

An Imprint of HarperCollinsPublishers

WHEN HENRY BROWN came into this world, his family sang.
Mama blew kisses on his soft, brown belly. Papa named him Henry, held him
high to the sky. Sisters and brothers tickled his toes.

Mama's cooking grew Henry tall. Papa's stories grew Henry smart. The whole family's love grew Henry strong. Even though they were slaves on Master's plantation.

As Henry worked 'neath Virginia's hot sun, he sang his workday song. Its lift, tote, toss-the-sack words sent strength to his arms.

In the garden, Henry sang his gather-up song. Its twist, snap, pick-a-pea words rang loud and clear.

At work time's end, Henry said, "Let's play hide-and-seek." His brothers and sisters laughed, shook their heads. "Your hidey-hole song always makes you too easy to find."

Most of Henry's songs were loud, but his favorite song wasn't. At sleep time, when his candle blew dark, Henry sang his freedom song. But silently, inside his head. Its freedom-land, family, stay-all-together words soothed Henry's greatest fear: the fear that Master would sell him.

Henry knew children who'd been sold from their mamas. He'd heard them crying at night. Henry's freedom song promised a place where families stayed together. Sometimes, freedom-song words tried to sneak from his mouth. That was when Henry bit his lips together, held the words inside. His master whipped slaves who sang freedom songs. He even sold them far, far away.

When Henry was almost grown, Master sent him to work in a tobacco factory in Richmond. There Henry sang a tobacco-work song. Its rustle, roll, chop-the-tobacco tune lightened his task. Henry seldom saw his family. From time to time, slaves carried word that Henry's family sent their love. On days when family-missing got too strong, Henry hummed his freedom song. It daydreamed him to freedom-land, where his family was free to visit him anytime.

One day, Henry met a woman named Nancy. Her smiles made his heart thump. His love songs made her cheeks glow. Finally, their masters gave them permission to marry. Henry and Nancy sang with joy.

Henry was papa proud when his first child was born. He named his son, held him high to the sky. At night, Henry sang him a cradle song. Its low, restful, close-your-eyes words rocked the baby to sleep.

Soon the baby had a brother and sisters. Henry pleased them with piggyback rides. He sweet-talked them with stories. He kissed away their tears and hurts and taught them right from wrong. Family songs hushed Henry's freedom song. And Henry's heart was full.

"Rustle, roll, chop the tobacco,"
Henry sang at work one day. Suddenly,
the factory door flew open. Henry's friend
rushed in. "Henry! Nancy's gone! Her
master sold her and your children!"
Henry's song died in his throat.

As Henry raced toward home, he passed a group of slaves in chains. Behind them heavy wagons rolled, loaded with sold-away children. "Papa, Papa!" Henry's heart stopped. His older son was in that first wagon. Henry fought to reach his son, to clutch him in his arms. But men held Henry back. By the time Henry pulled free, his son was gone.

A woman in chains jumped aside from the others. Nancy! Henry clasped her hands. He held on tight and walked for miles, until men tore him away.

For weeks, silence filled Henry's house. "Poor Henry. No songs left in his heart," said a neighbor, shaking her head. But she was wrong. Henry *did* still have a song. His freedom song. And its think, plan, take-yourself-to-freedom-land words were getting stronger every day. There were folks in freedom-land who could help him find Nancy and the children.

Secret friends, in hushed voices, told Henry, "Ask Samuel Smith 'bout the road to freedom-land. He knows the way of the Underground Railroad."

Henry waved Samuel to a dark, alone corner. "Samuel, I got to get free. Will you help?"

"Yes—let's work on a plan," Samuel replied.

A stack of boxes behind Samuel's dry goods store got Henry thinking. Thinking up a daring plan that no slave had ever tried. *Samuel ships boxes to freedom-land,* Henry thought. *Why couldn't he ship me, too?*

Late at night, Henry sawed secret wood and hammered secret nails, working hard on a sturdy wooden box. He drilled three holes for air, then lined the inside with soft, thick cloth.

"What will you do so your master won't miss you?" Samuel asked.

The next day, at work, Henry sang his tobacco-work song. Rustle, roll, chop the tobacco. Rustle, roll, chop the tobacco. Rustle, roll—Henry clenched his teeth and—CHOP! But not tobacco. This time he chopped his finger. Right down to the bone. When Tobacco Boss saw the blood, he sent Henry home. "And don't you come back till that cut is healed!"

"Yes, sir," said Henry.

"I won't come back."

Early next morning, Henry filled a pouch with water and curled up in his box. With five hickory loops, Henry's friend James, a free black man, wrapped the lid down tight. Samuel marked Henry's box THIS SIDE UP WITH CARE. He addressed the label to William Johnson, a freedom-loving man in Pennsylvania, a freedom-land state.

New words in Henry's freedom song—hush, be still, don't-make-a-sound words—kept Henry company on the way to the train station. When they arrived, James tapped softly on Henry's box. *Tap, tap.* James's secret knock asked, "Are you all right?" *Tap.* Henry's one-knock answer meant *I'm fine.*

Men swung Henry's box into a railway car. The train wheels added new words to Henry's freedom tune. Each *clickety-clack* beat of its *clickety-clack* words carried Henry closer to freedom. But Henry's journey was a long one. The air in Henry's box got warm. And then got even warmer. Sweat ran like tears down Henry's cheeks. He was sure his box was shrinking. Could he bear the squeeze much longer?

Henry's box was loaded—upside down—onto the deck of a steamboat. Henry's body pressed down on his head. His eyes bulged. The veins in his forehead swelled as big around as his little finger. Now Henry's freedom song had Lord-give-me-strength words.

Just when Henry thought he would break, voices spoke beside him. "What do you think is in this box?" A foot kicked Henry's box. "Mail, likely. Let's open it and see." Henry's heart raced harder as fingers pried at the box. But James's hickory loops held firm. "Stop! Someone's coming. Turn the box. We'll sit on it instead." When they tipped him onto his side, Henry almost sang, *"Hallelujah!"* But he didn't. He stayed silent.

Finally, Henry's box swung back to the bed of another wagon. Henry heard the jingle of a horse's harness and a driver yell, "Giddyap." The wagon lurched forward, and Henry's box started to slide. Henry braced himself, but there was nothing he could do. *C-r-a-c-k!* His box crashed down. Henry's head slammed wooden sides, and that was all Henry knew.

Swaying and a gentle thud roused Henry back awake. He listened for voices, for any sound that would tell him where he was. *Thud, thud, thud.* Footsteps, followed by . . . silence. *Am I safe?* Henry wondered. *What should I do?* His freedom song cautioned him with stay-still, don't-move, wait-to-be-sure words.

Then, *Tap, tap. Tap.*
The secret code knock! *Tap.*
Henry knocked back in reply.

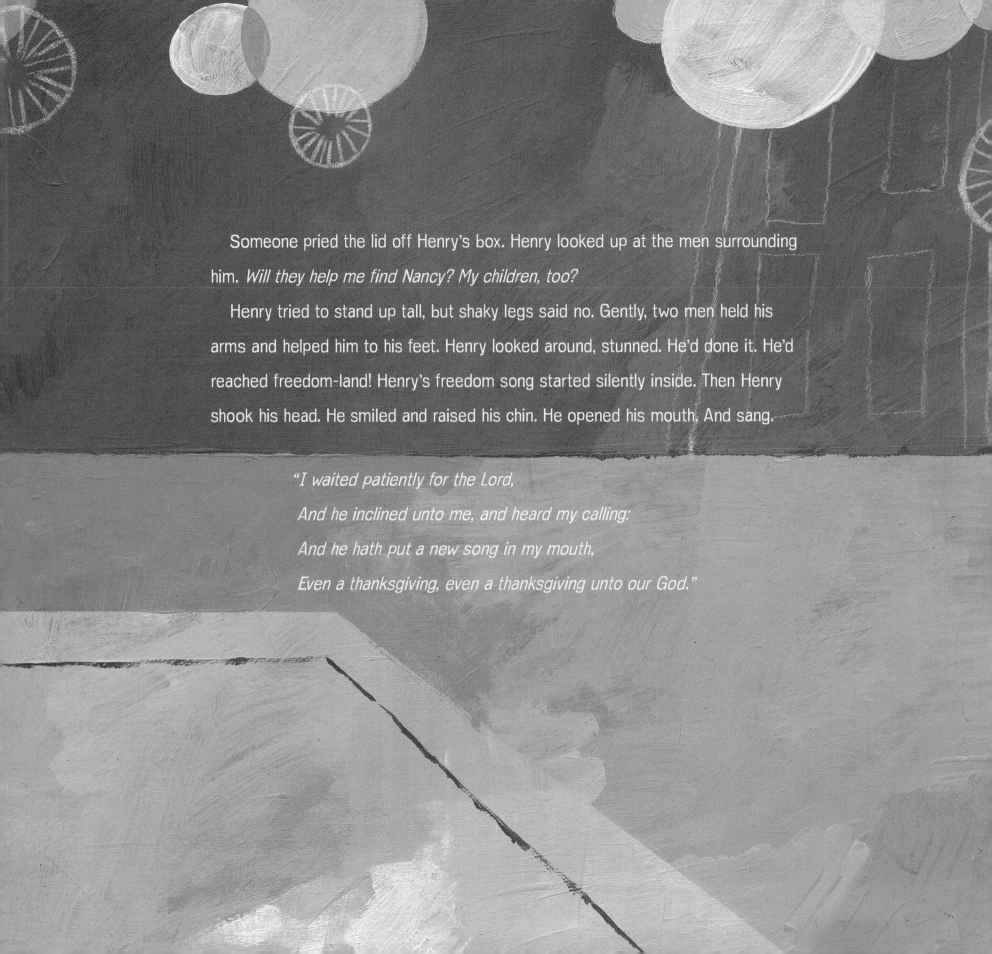

Someone pried the lid off Henry's box. Henry looked up at the men surrounding him. *Will they help me find Nancy? My children, too?*

Henry tried to stand up tall, but shaky legs said no. Gently, two men held his arms and helped him to his feet. Henry looked around, stunned. He'd done it. He'd reached freedom-land! Henry's freedom song started silently inside. Then Henry shook his head. He smiled and raised his chin. He opened his mouth. And sang.

> *"I waited patiently for the Lord,*
>
> *And he inclined unto me, and heard my calling:*
>
> *And he hath put a new song in my mouth,*
>
> *Even a thanksgiving, even a thanksgiving unto our God."*

HENRY "BOX" BROWN was a real person. He was born about 1815, on a plantation near Richmond, Virginia. After his arrival in Philadelphia, in March 1849, Henry gave lectures about life in slavery and his amazing escape. But he wasn't the only person who "talked" about it. James McKim, who received Henry's box at the Anti-Slavery Office, sent a letter about Henry's escape to a friend, and he made a copy of it for his records. That copy still survives and is in the New-York Historical Society's Slavery Collection. One way we learn about past events is by reading letters such as this one.

I first heard about Henry Brown many years ago, when I was in college. Being a choir member and a music lover, I understood how a burst of song might express the intense emotions that Henry felt upon being freed from his small prison. Much later, in 2003, while reading Jeffrey Ruggles's excellent book *The Unboxing of Henry Brown*, I was fascinated to learn that Henry had been a member of his church choir for many years. Ruggles explained that singing and music played an important part in the lives of slaves. And I began to imagine: What other songs might Henry have sung? As I wrote my story, I tried to make song a part of Henry's daily life, including his work at the tobacco factory. For that song, I did make one small change to Henry's tale. In real life, he burned his hand with acid. The rhythm of my tobacco song needed the strength of a chop. I hope that Henry, a storyteller in his own right, would understand.

In 1850, Henry moved to England, driven by fear of recapture under the Fugitive Slave Act. There, Henry continued speaking out against slavery. Eventually, his trail disappears into history. To date, no one has discovered whether he was ever reunited with Nancy or their children.

Anti-Slavery Office
Phil^a March 26, 1849

Dear Gay,

Here is a man who has been the hero of one of the most extraordinary achievements I ever heard of. He came to me on Saturday morning last in a box tightly hooped, marked "this side up" by <u>overland express, from the city of Richmond</u>!! Did you ever hear of any thing in your life to beat that? . . . To appreciate fully the boldness and risk of the achievement you ought to see the box and hear all the circumstances. The box is 3 ft 2 inches long; 2 ft 8 in deep; & 1 ft 11 in wide [with] but the very slightest crevice to admit the air. . . . The "this side up" on the box was not regarded, and he was twice put with his head downwards. . . . The first time he succeeded in shifting his position; but the second time was on board the steamboat, where people were sitting and standing about the box, and where any motions inside would have been overheard and have led to discovery; he was therefore obliged to keep his position <u>for 20 miles</u>. This nearly killed him. He says the veins in his temples were as thick as his finger.

I had been expecting him for several days, and was in mortal fear all the time lest his arrival should only be a signal for calling in the coroner. You can better imagine than I can describe my sensations, when in answer to my rap on the box and question—"all right?" the prompt response came "all right sir."

The man weighs 200 lbs and is about 5 ft 8 in in height, and as you will see a noble looking fellow.— He will tell you the whole story. . . .

And now I have one request to make: for Heaven's sake don't publish this affair or allow it to be published. It would . . . prevent all others from escaping in the same way.

Yours truly,
J. M. McKim

❧ A copy of this letter is in the Collection of The New-York Historical Society. You can read the whole letter and see an image of it on the web at http://documents.nytimes.com/when-special-delivery-meant-deliverance-for-a-fugitive-slave, and you can visit the Society at www.nyhistory.org.

For Candace Fleming and Richard Starke, who heard
the rhythm of Henry's story and felt the soul in his song.
—S.M.W.

For Sally, Anne, and Martha.
And for you and your freedom song.
—S.Q.

Freedom Song: The Story of Henry "Box" Brown
Text copyright © 2012 by Sally M. Walker
Illustrations copyright © 2012 by Sean Qualls
All rights reserved.
Manufactured in China.
No part of this book may be used or reproduced in any manner whatsoever without written permission
except in the case of brief quotations embodied in critical articles and reviews.
For information address HarperCollins Children's Books, a division of HarperCollins Publishers,
10 East 53rd Street, New York, NY 10022.
www.harperchildrens.com

Library of Congress Cataloging-in-Publication Data is available.
Library of Congress catalog card number: 2010024448
ISBN 978-0-06-058310-1 (trade bdg.) — ISBN 978-0-06-058311-8 (lib. bdg.)

Typography by Martha Rago
12 13 14 15   SCP   10 9 8 7 6 5 4 3 2

First Edition